I0463660

HALLOWEEN HORRORS

ADULT COLORING BOOK

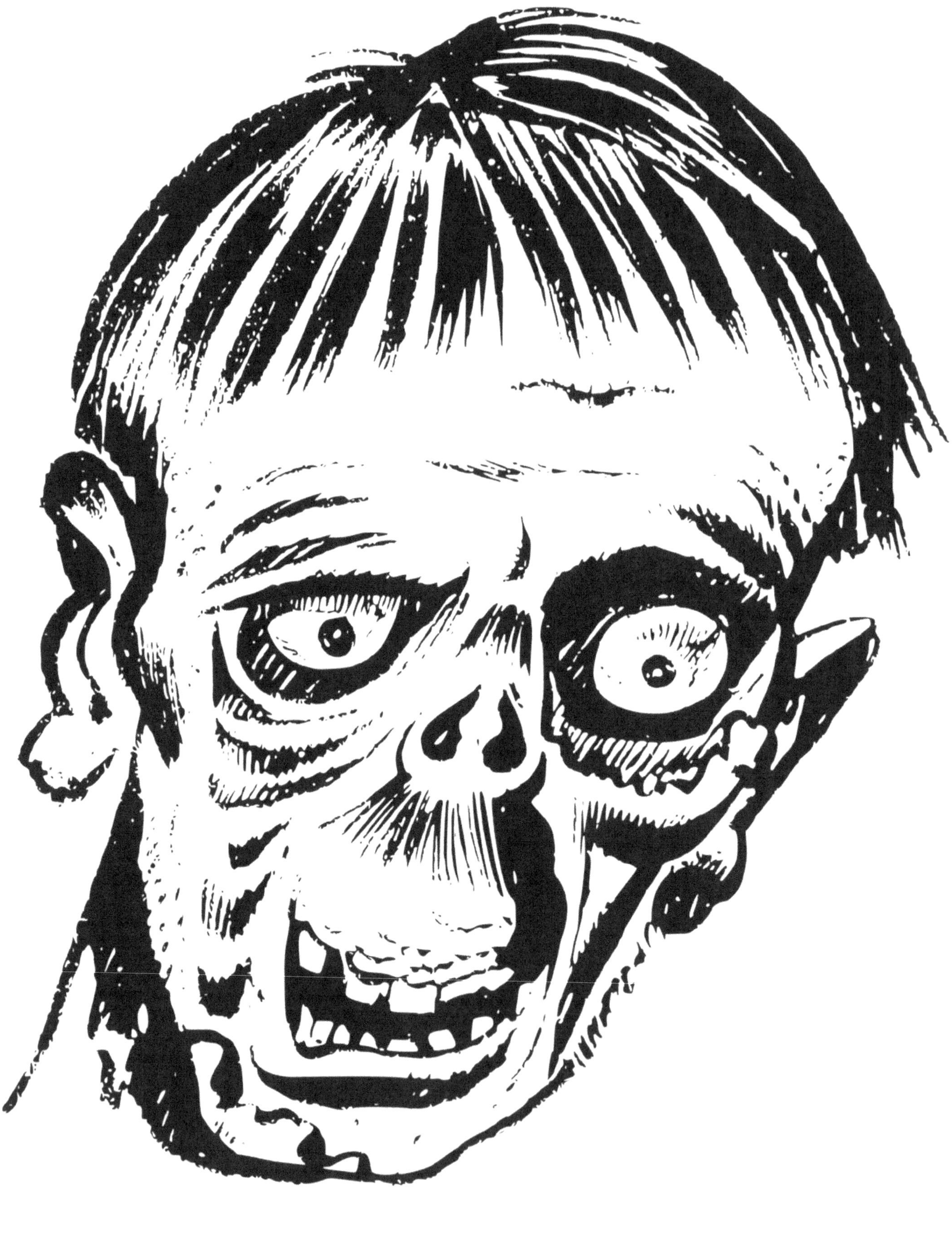

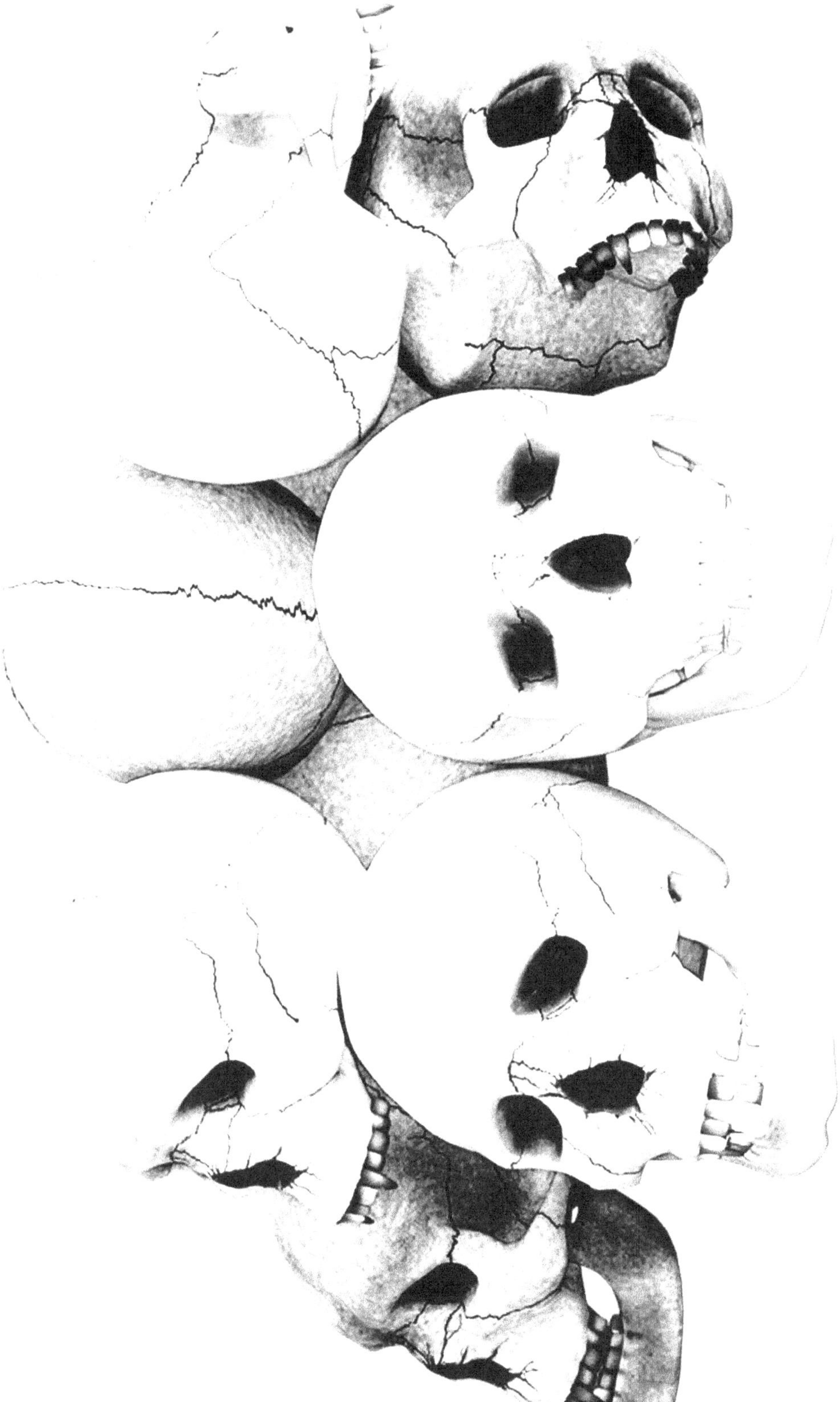

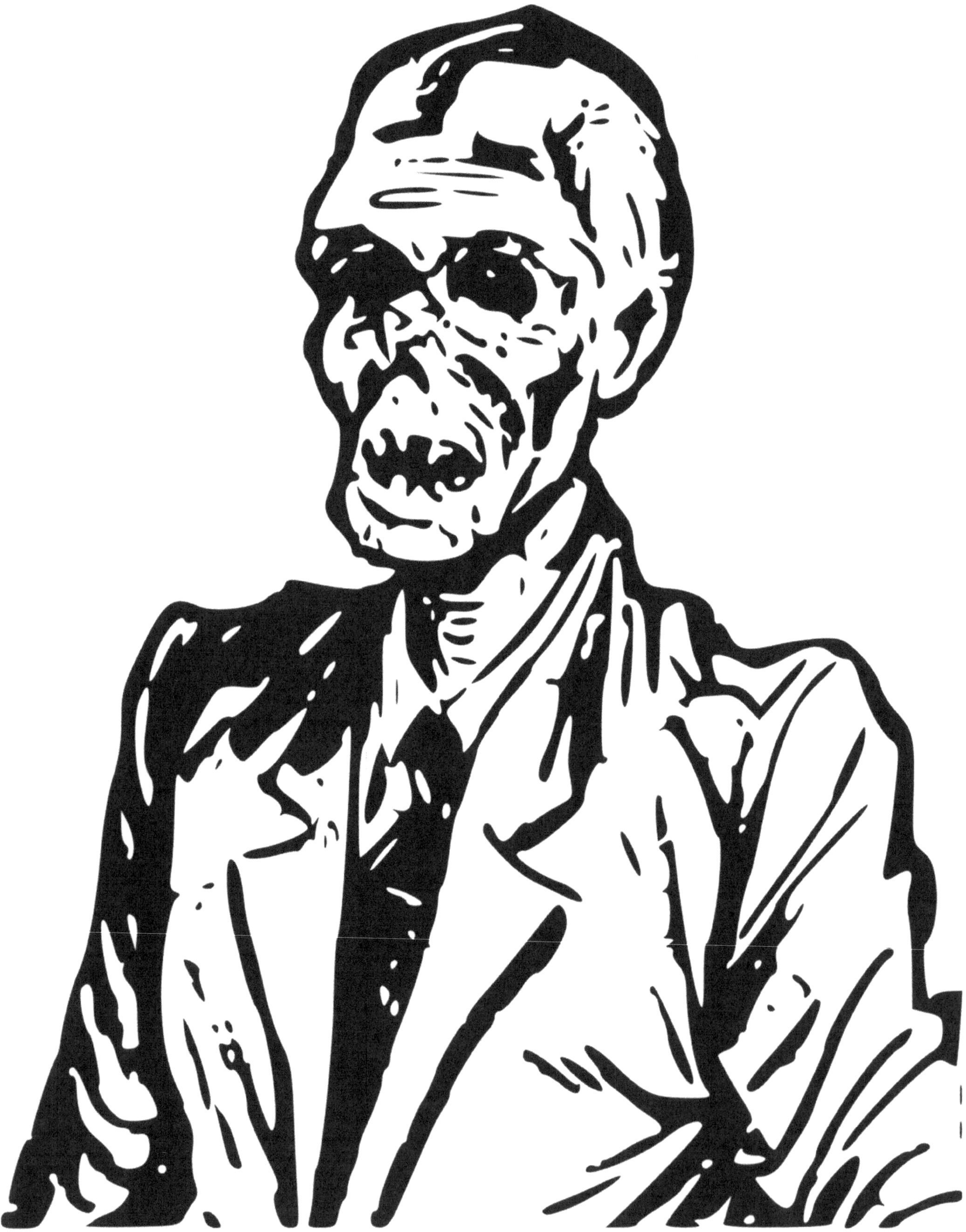

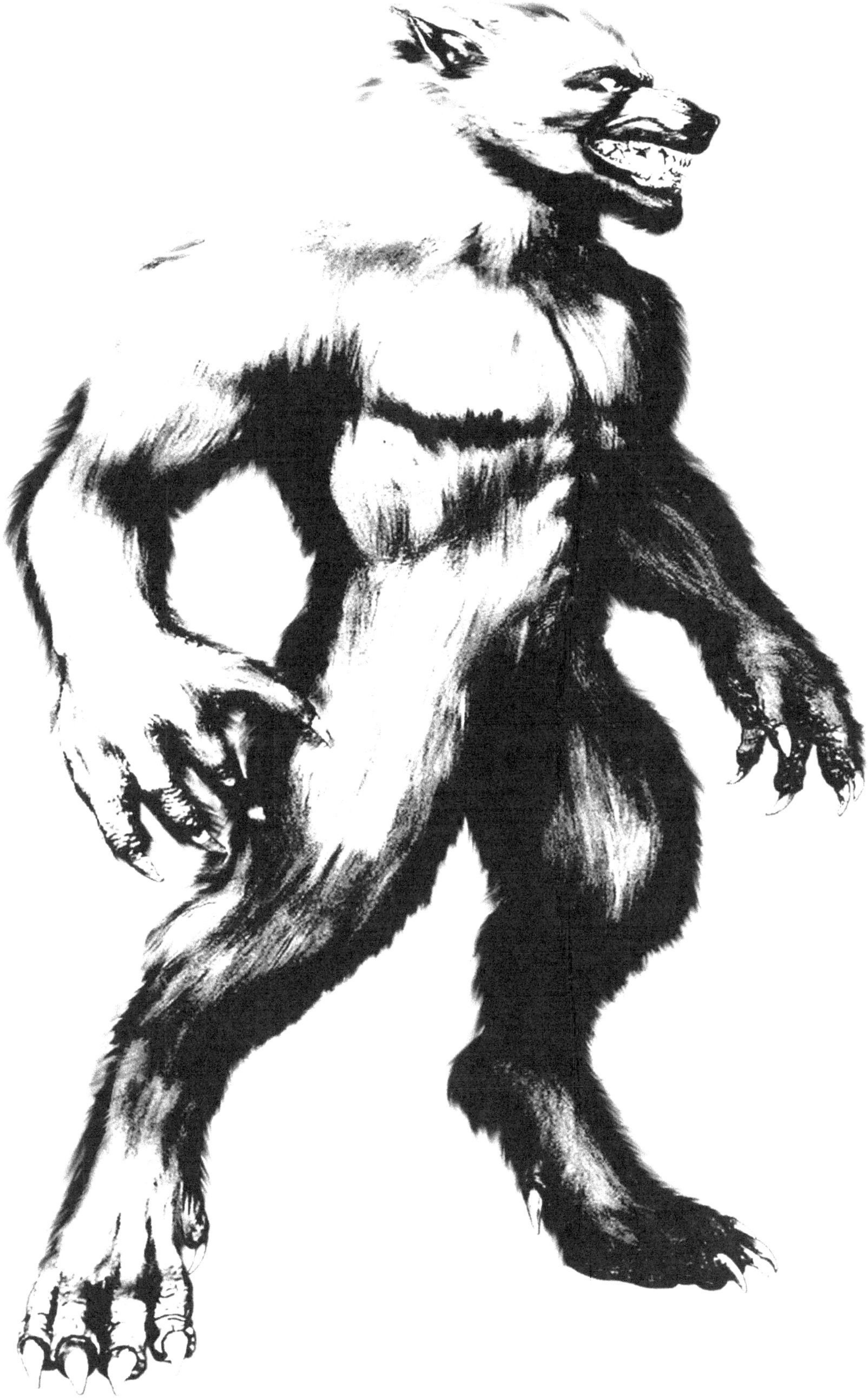

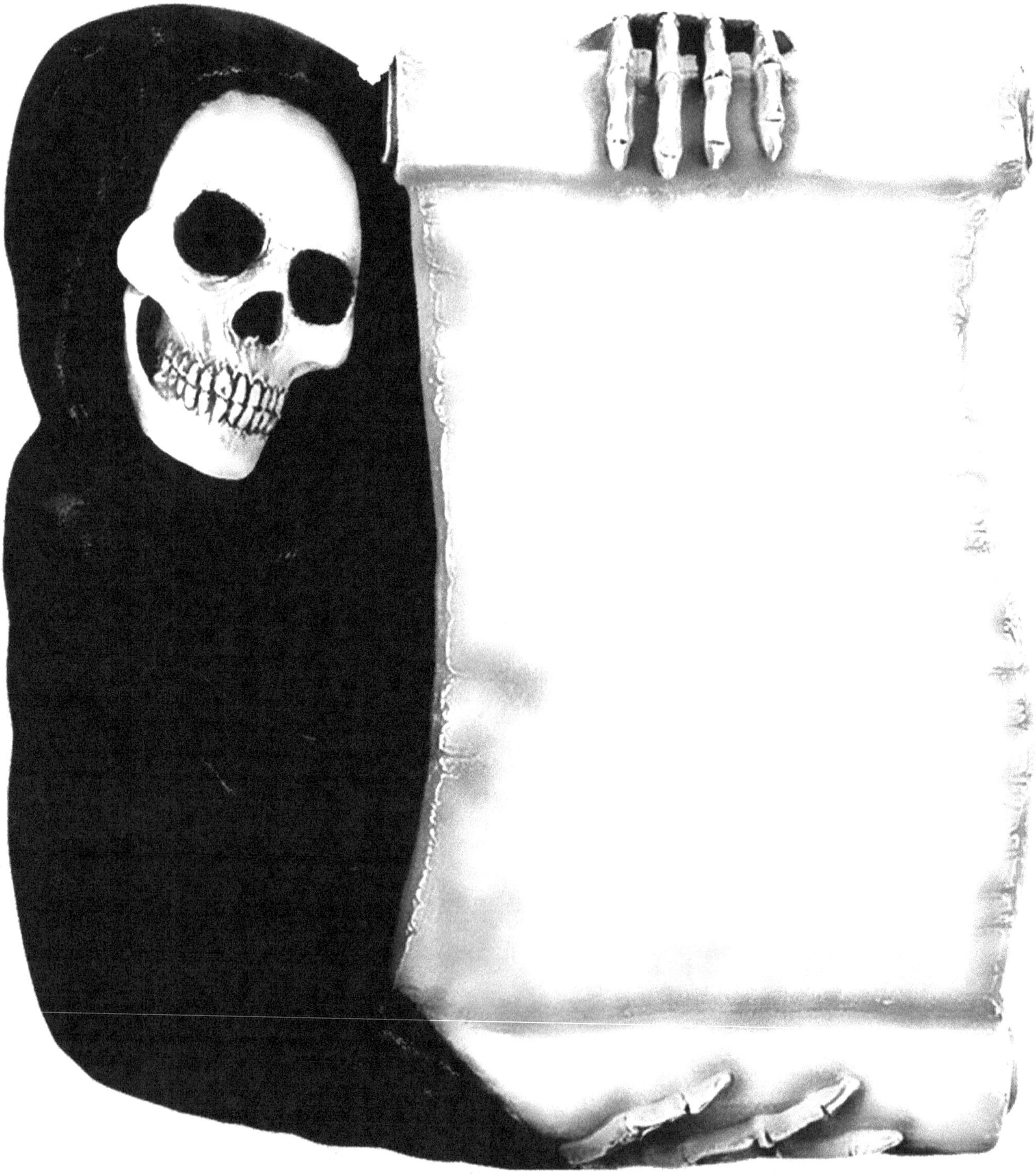

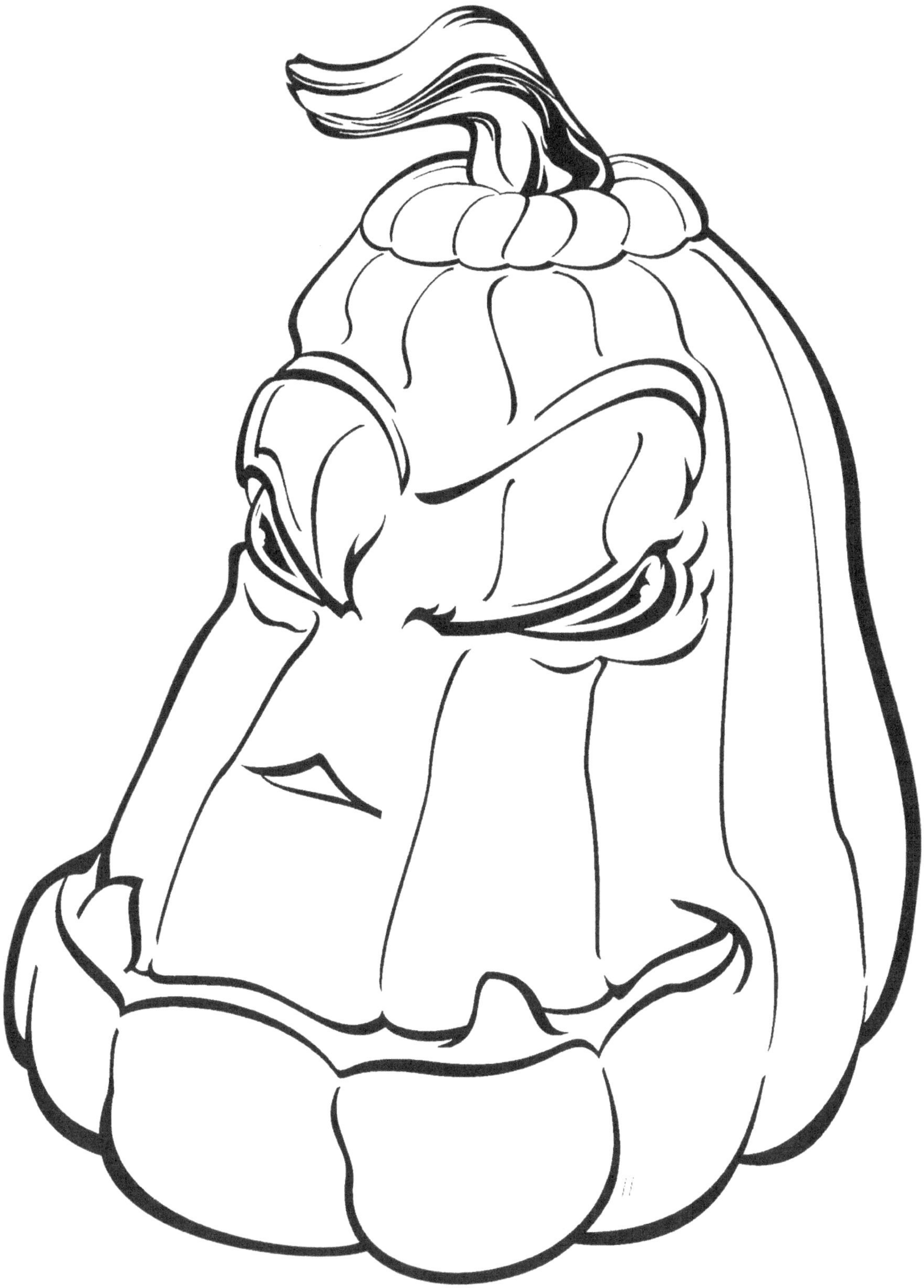

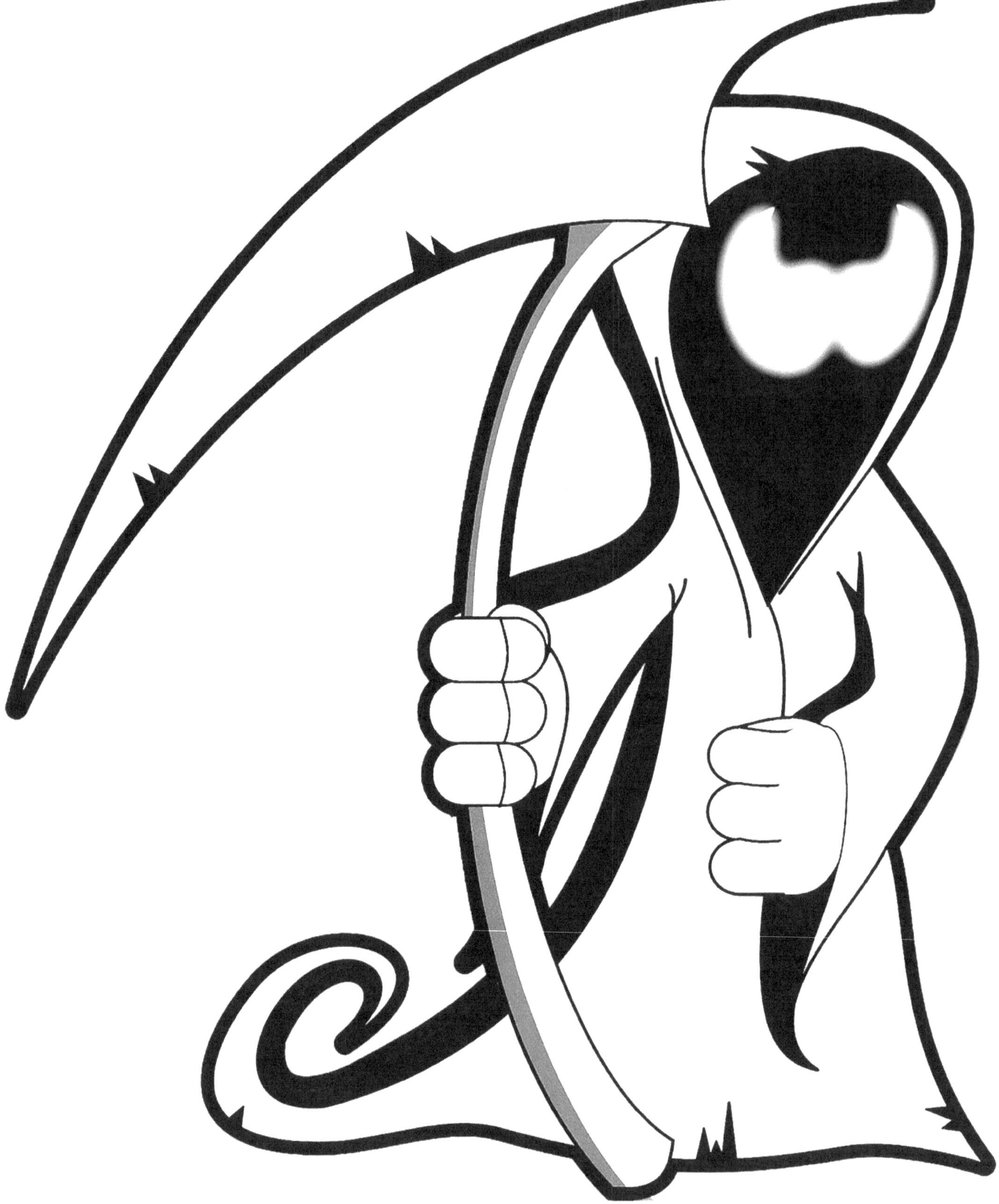

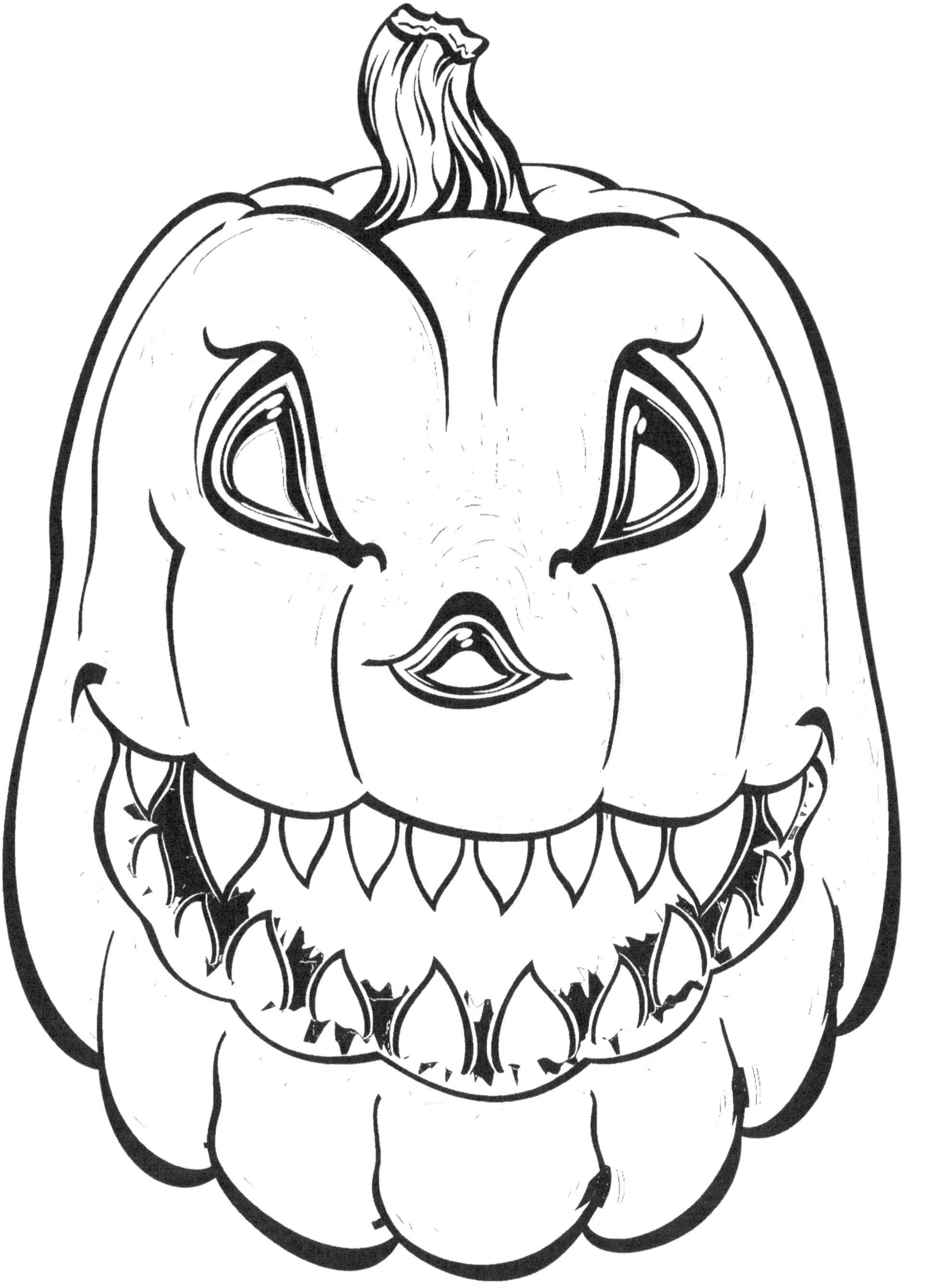

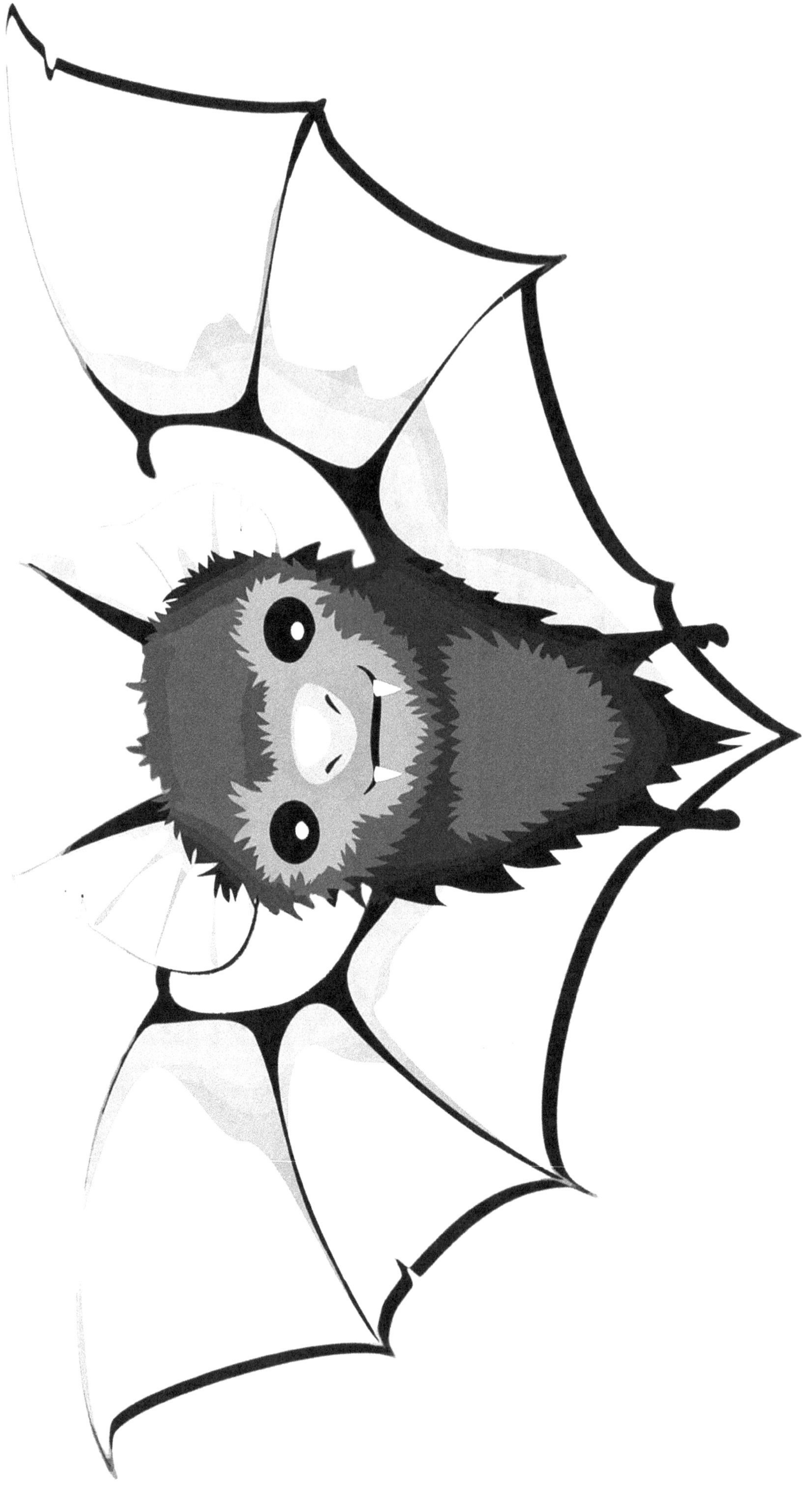

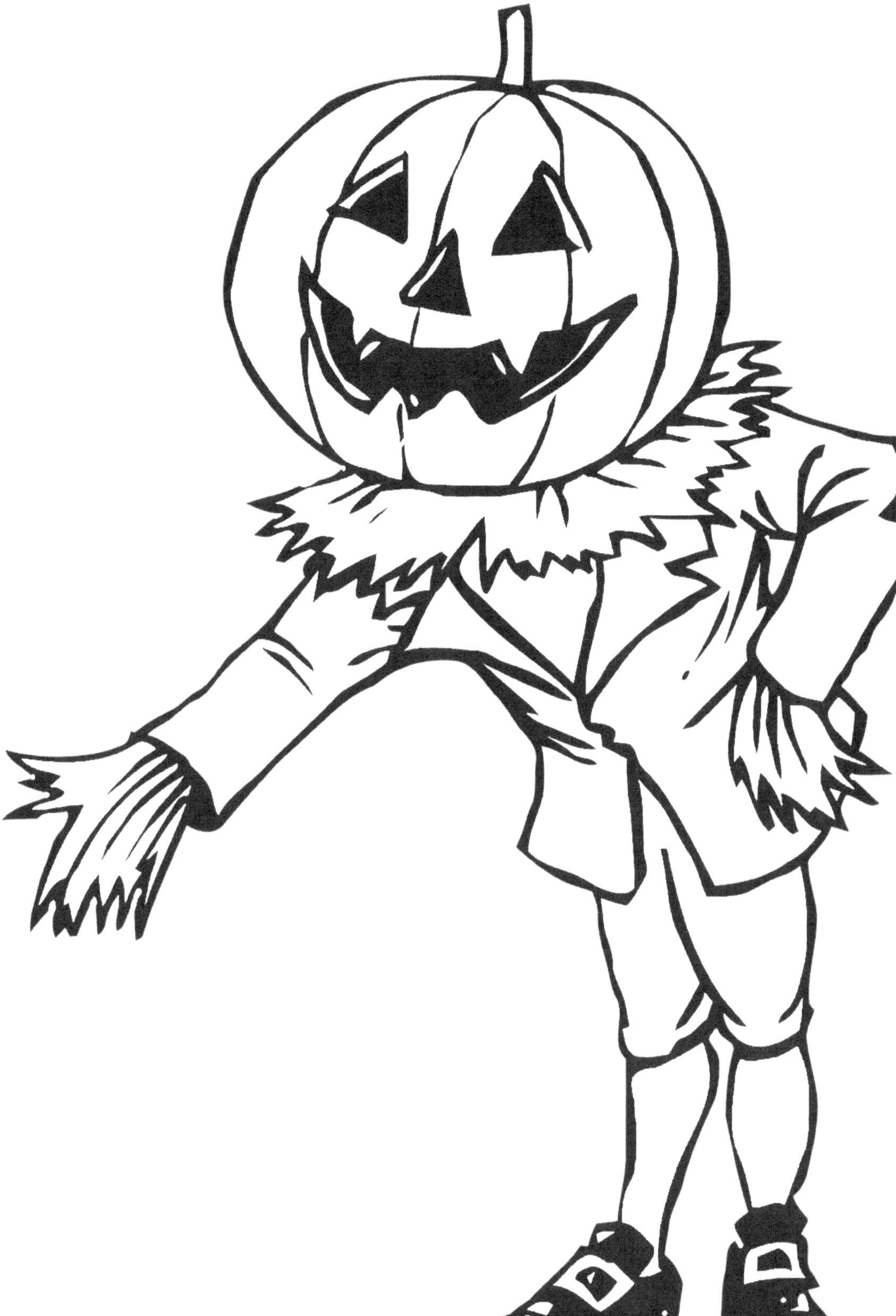

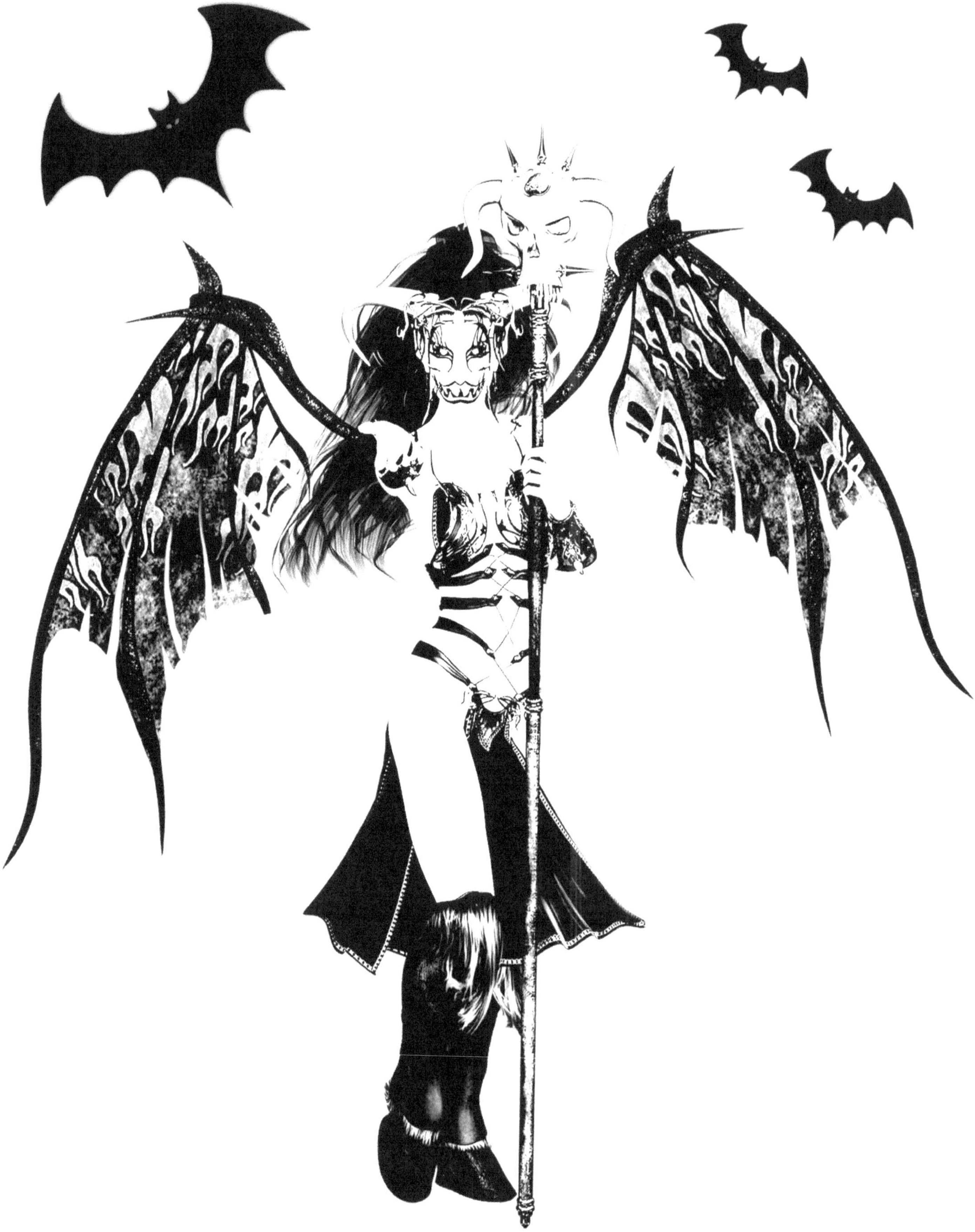

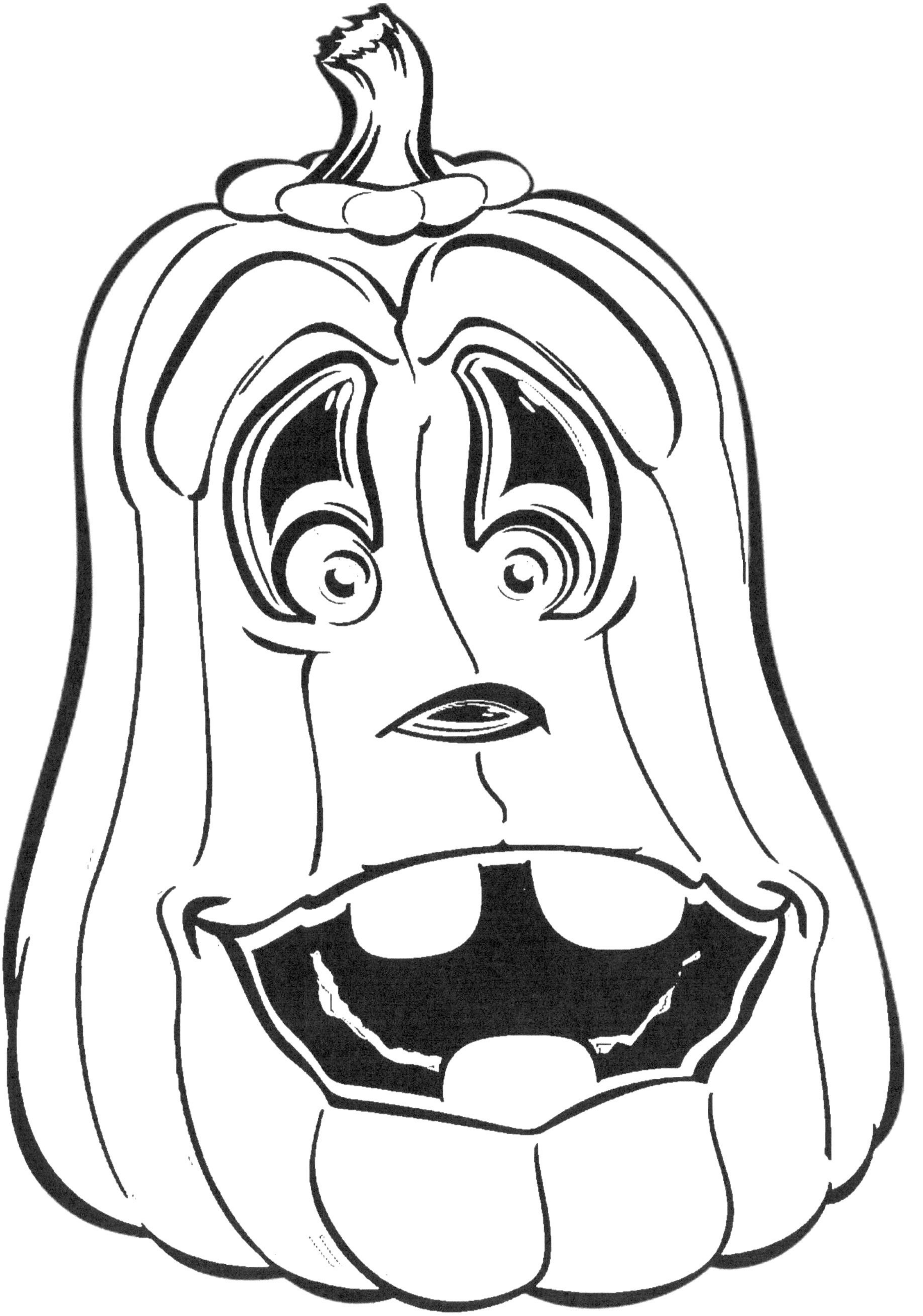

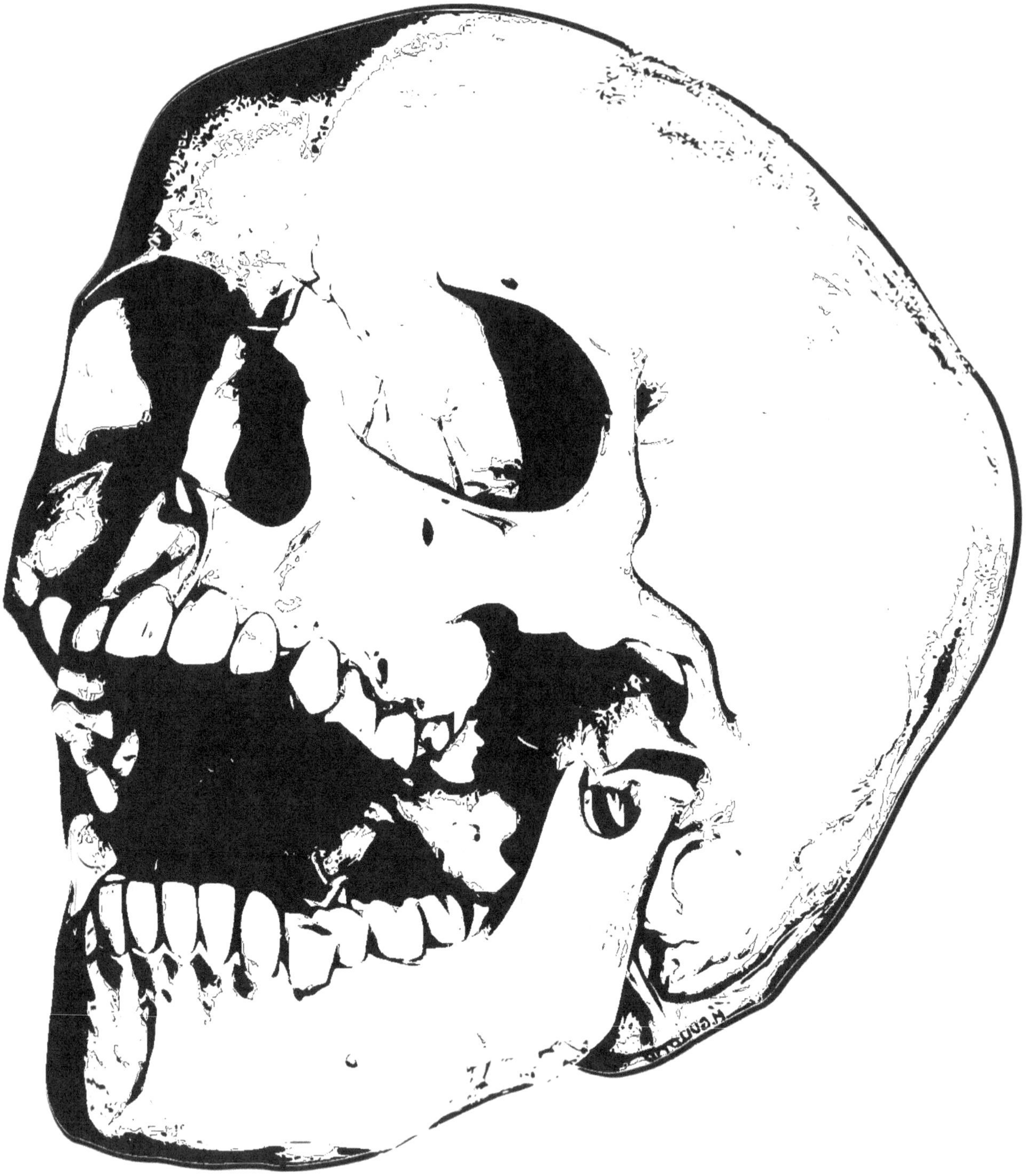

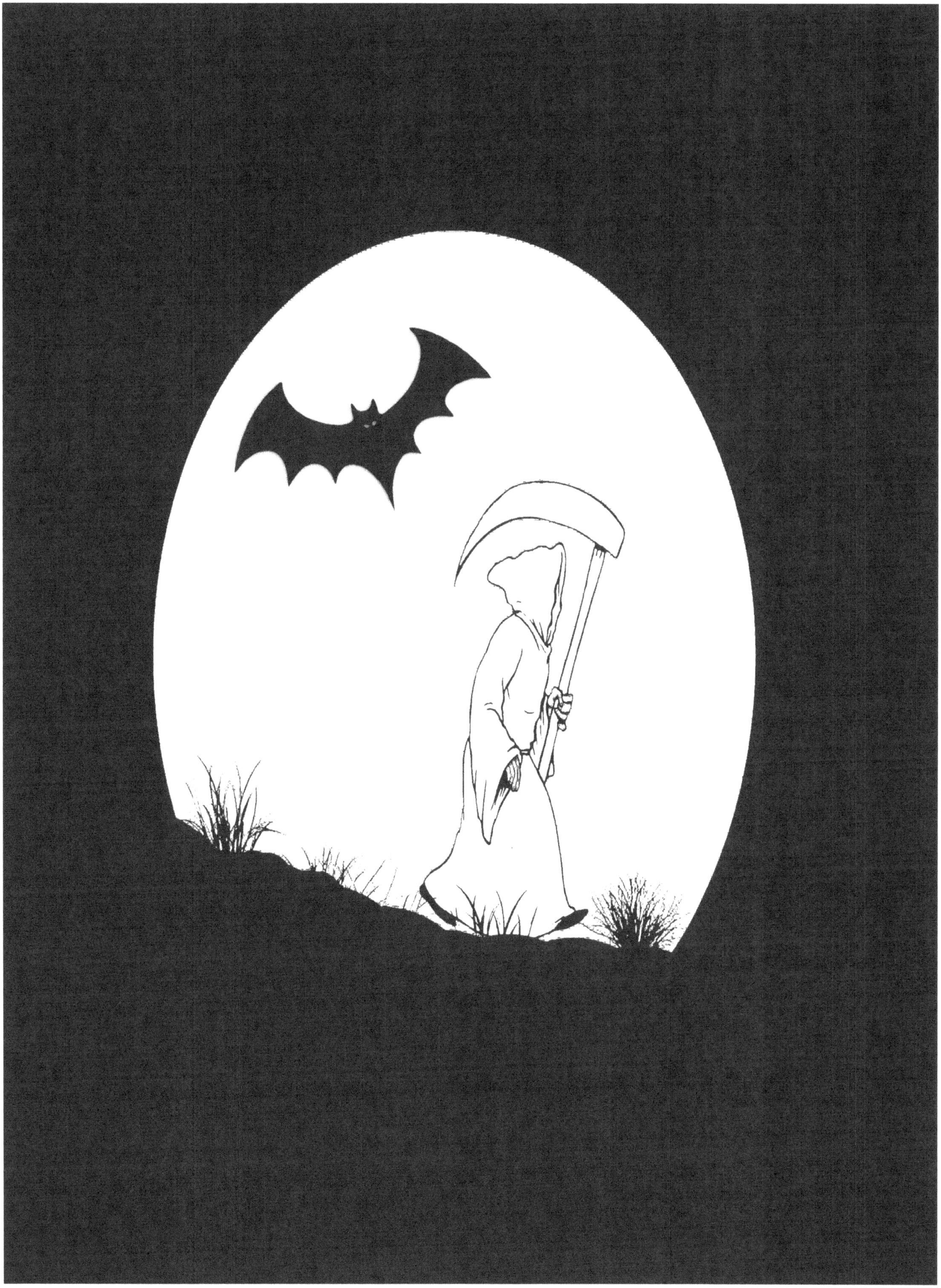

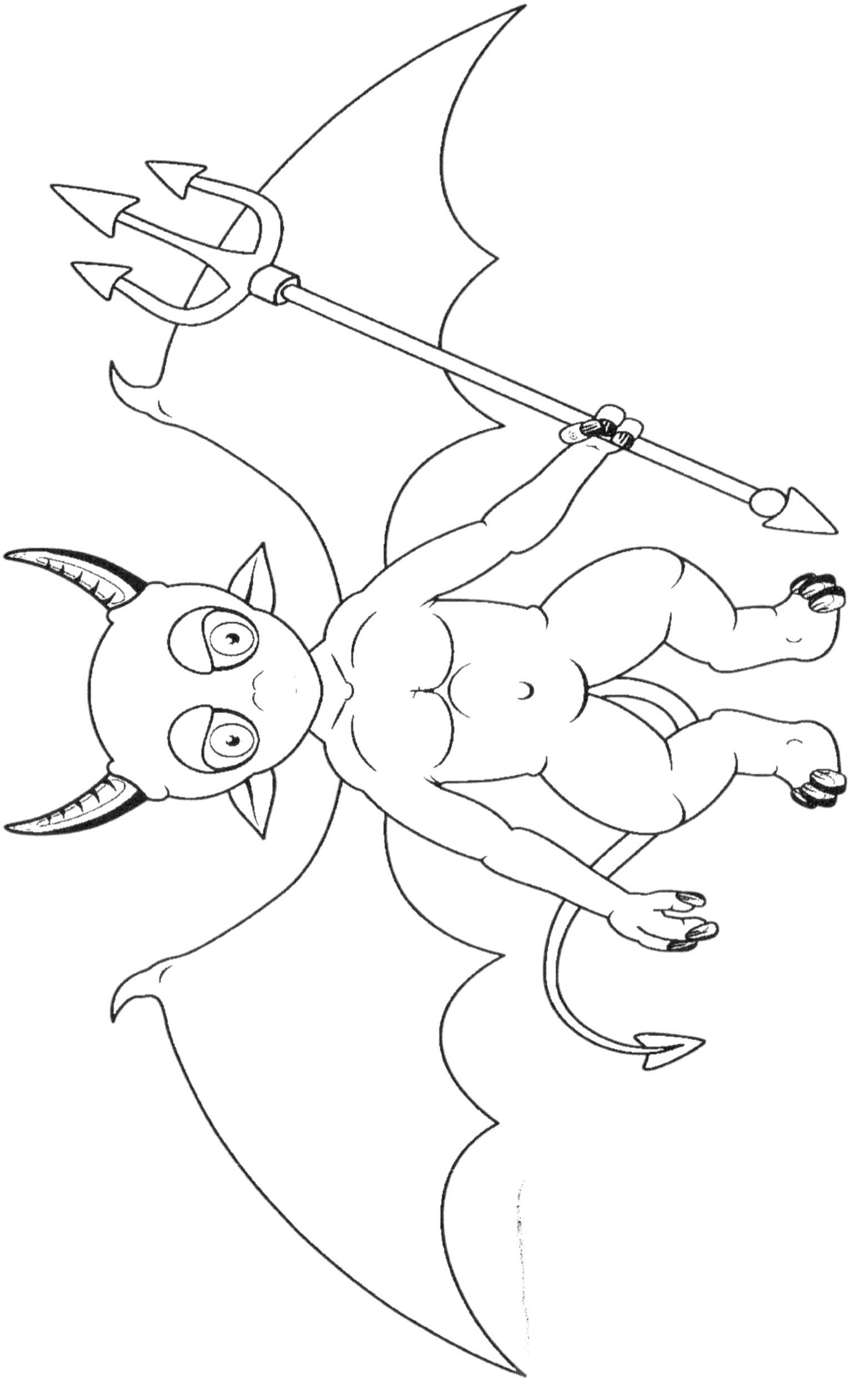

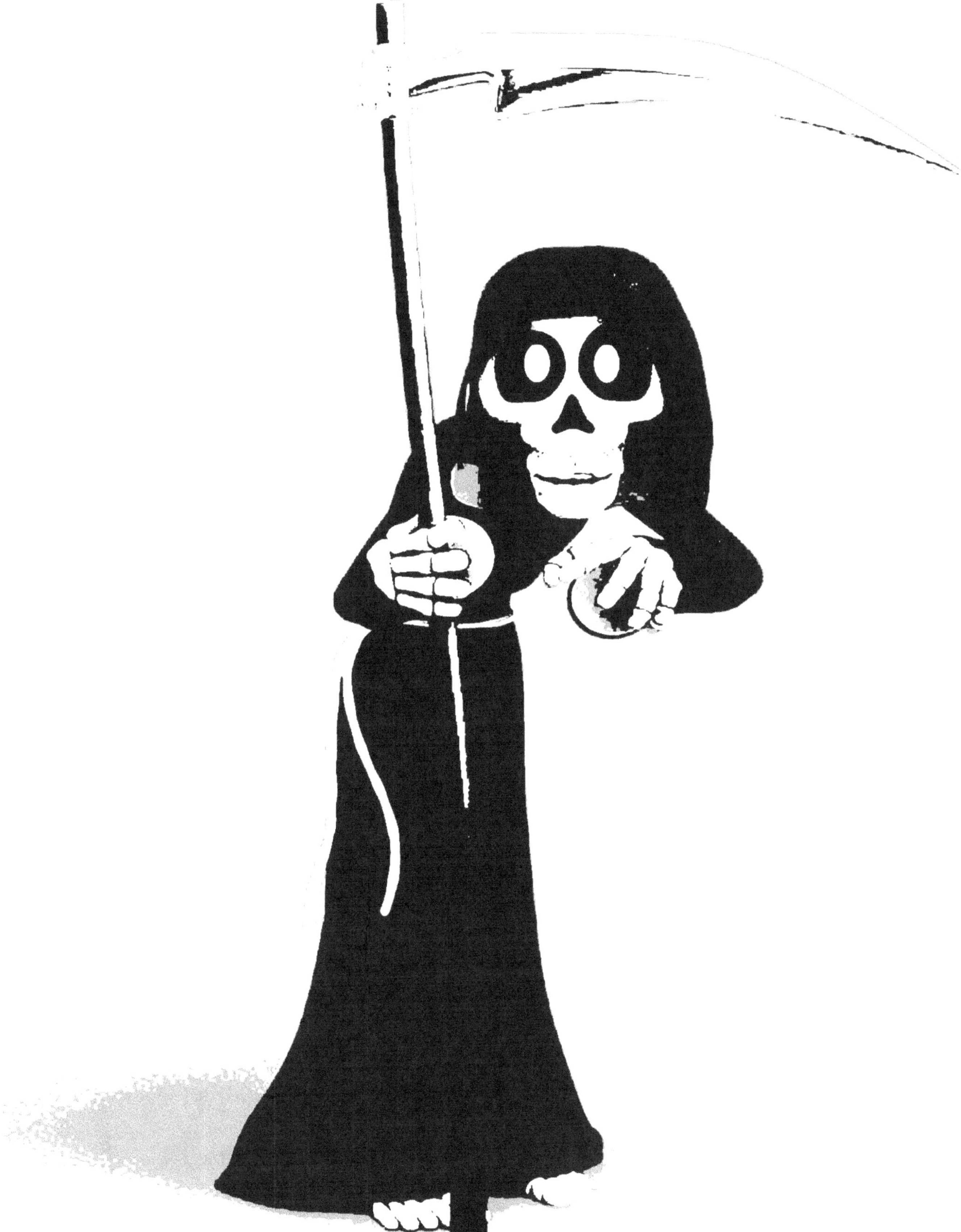

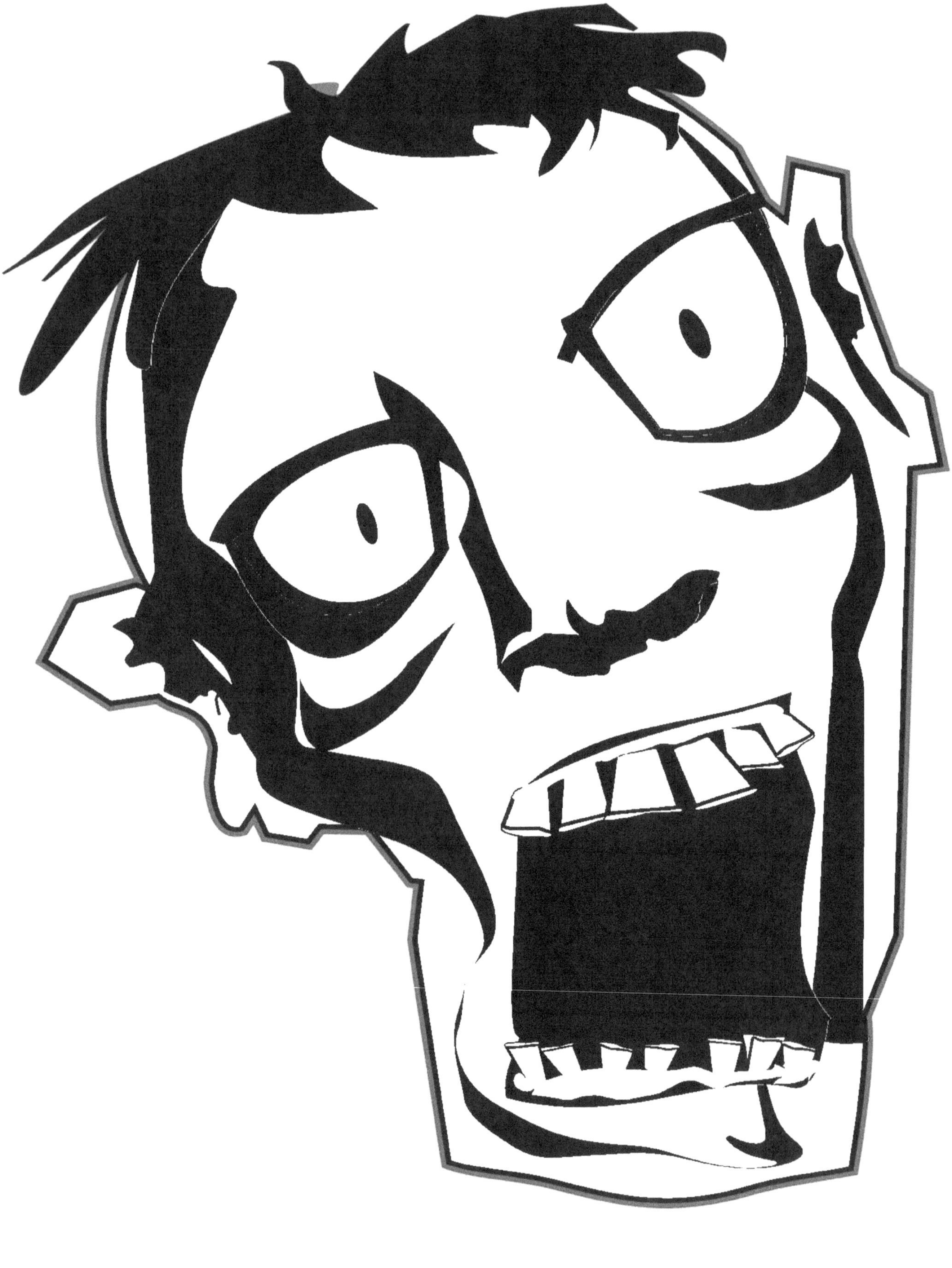

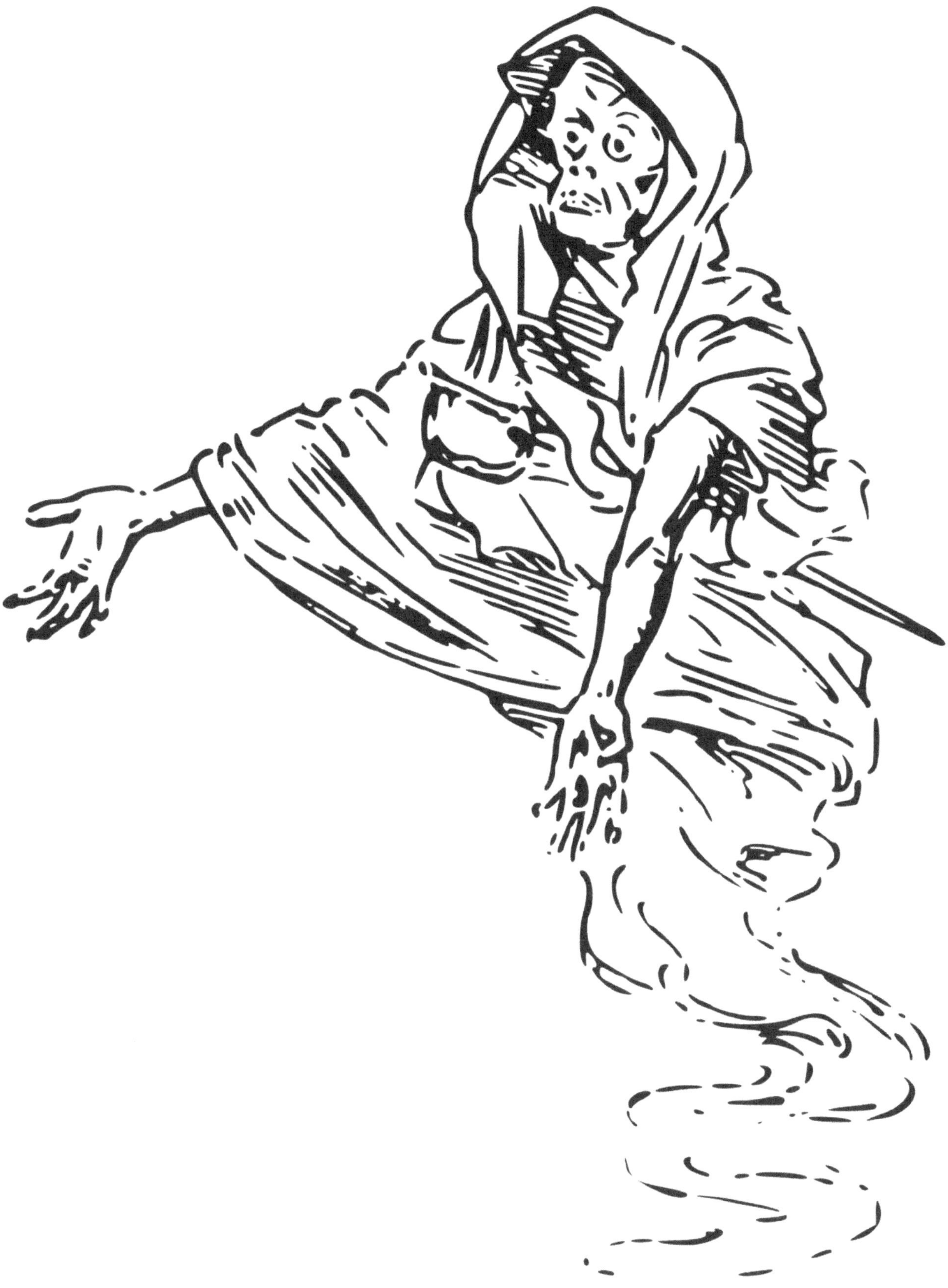

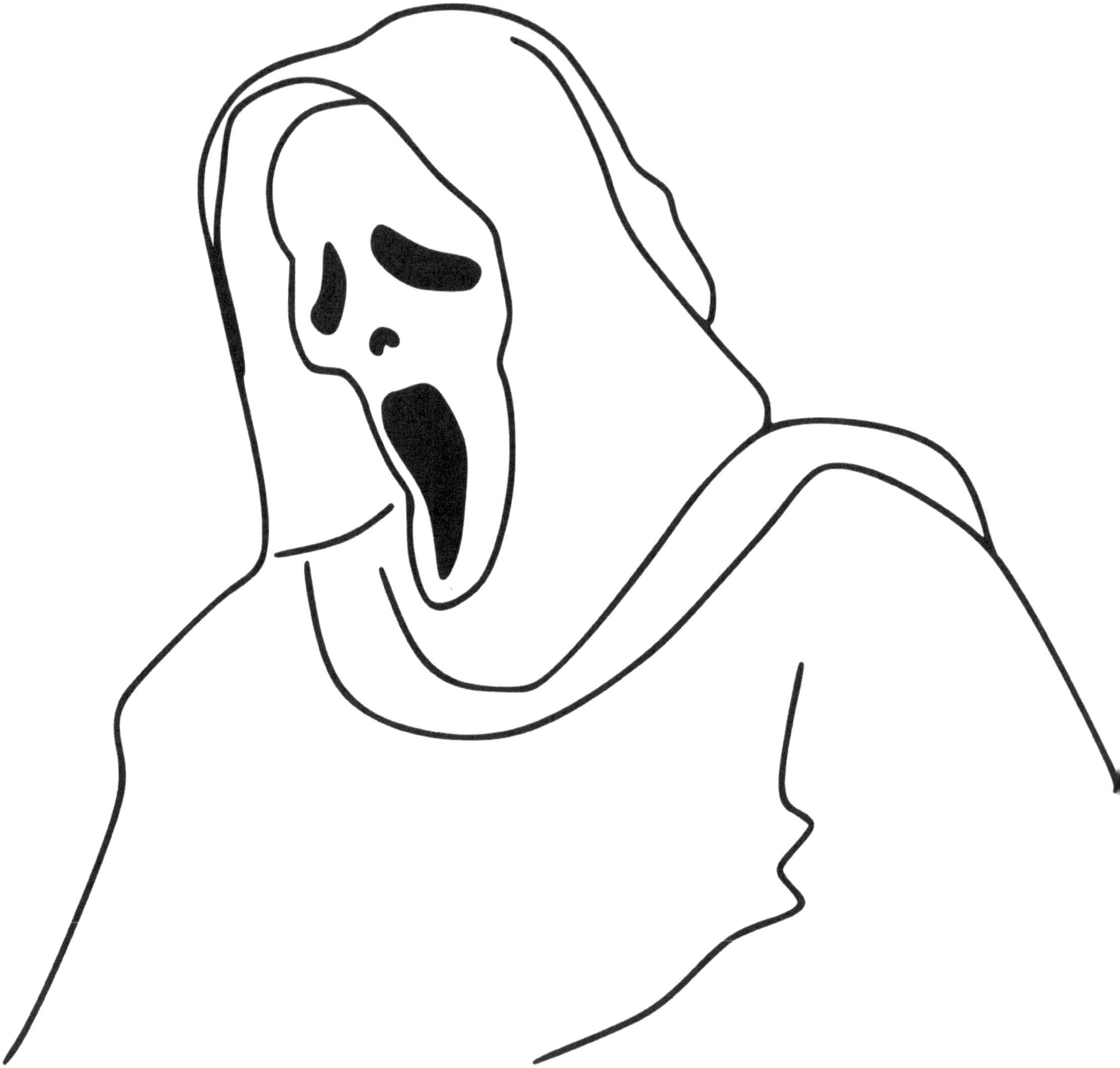

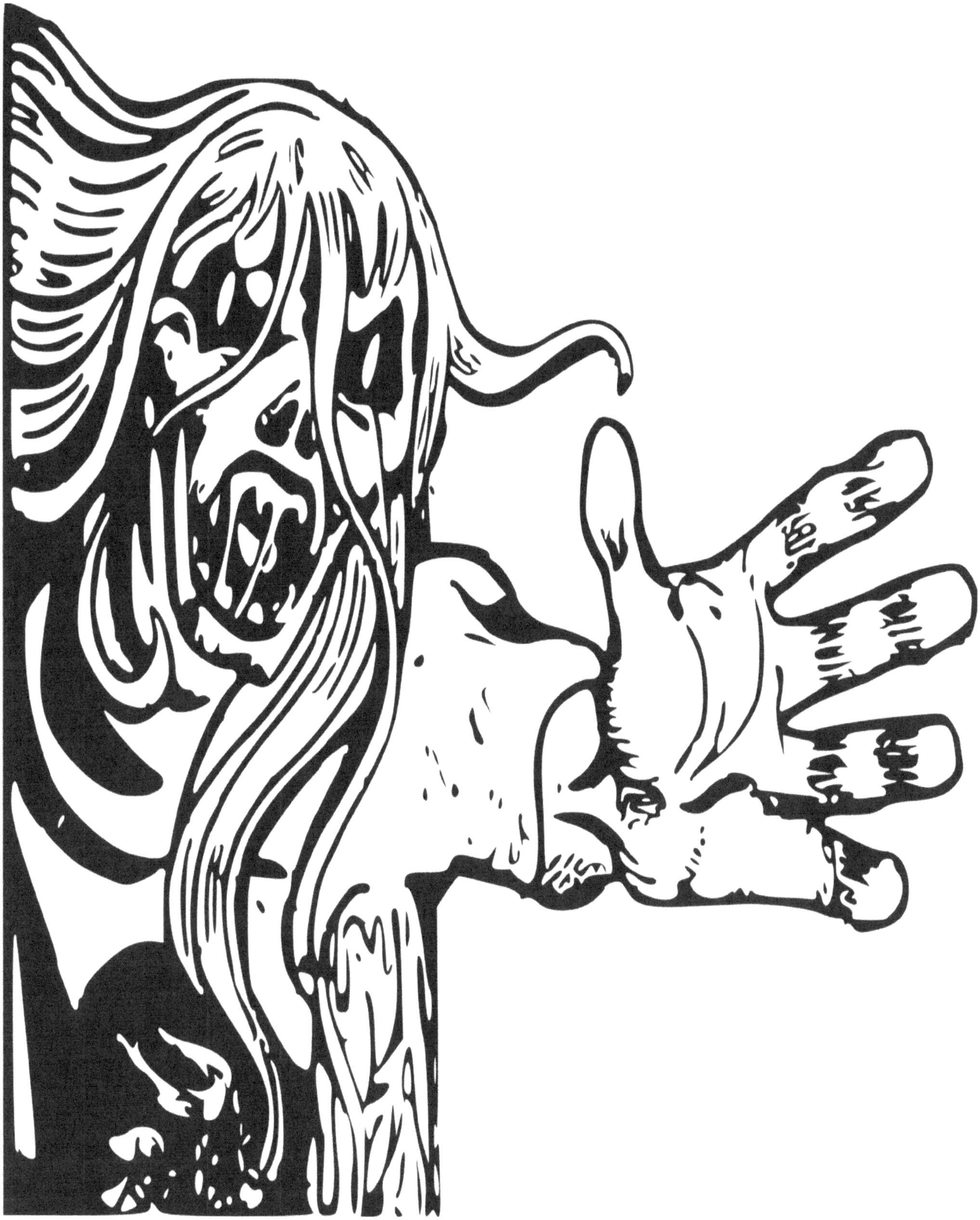

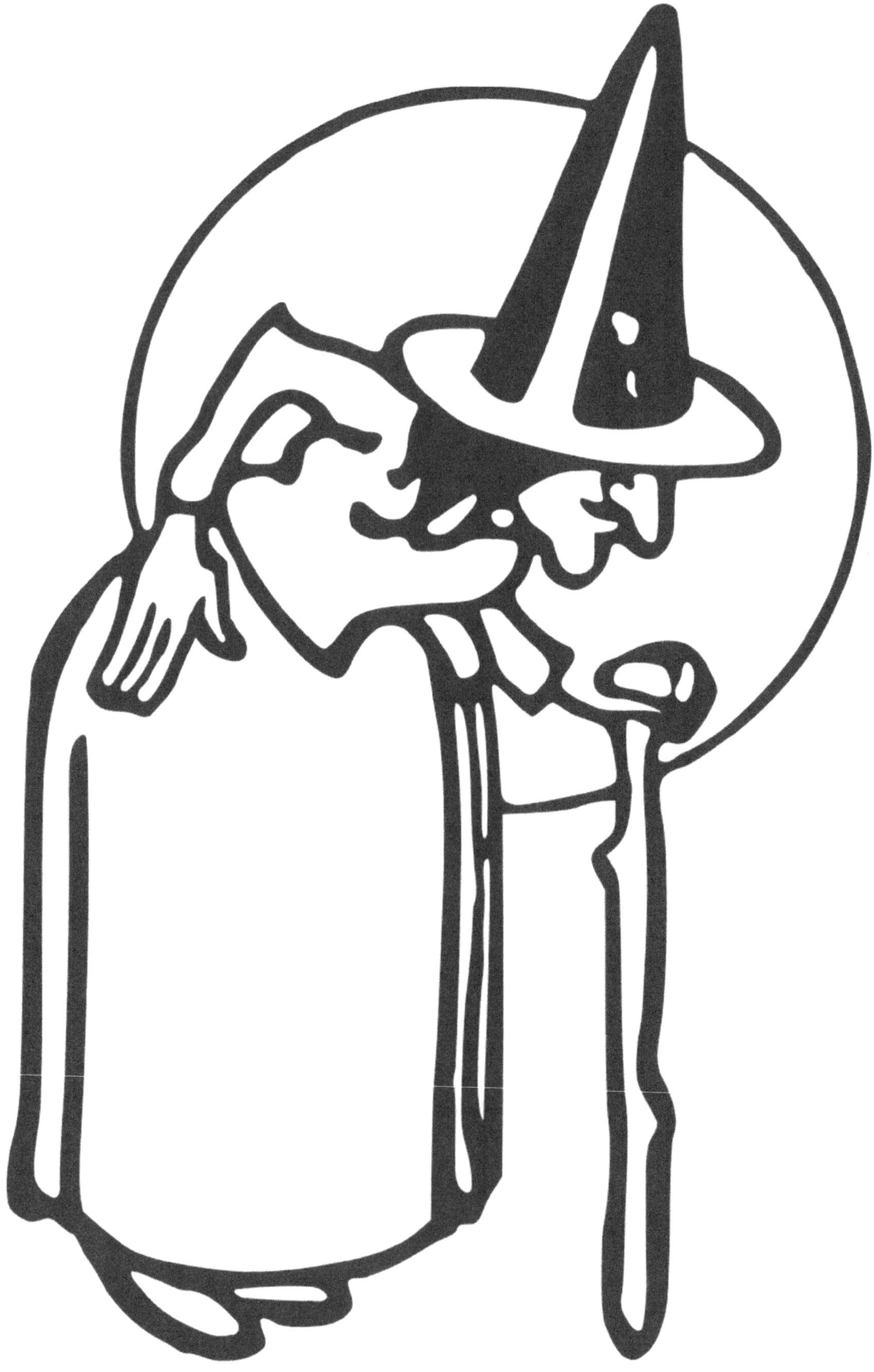

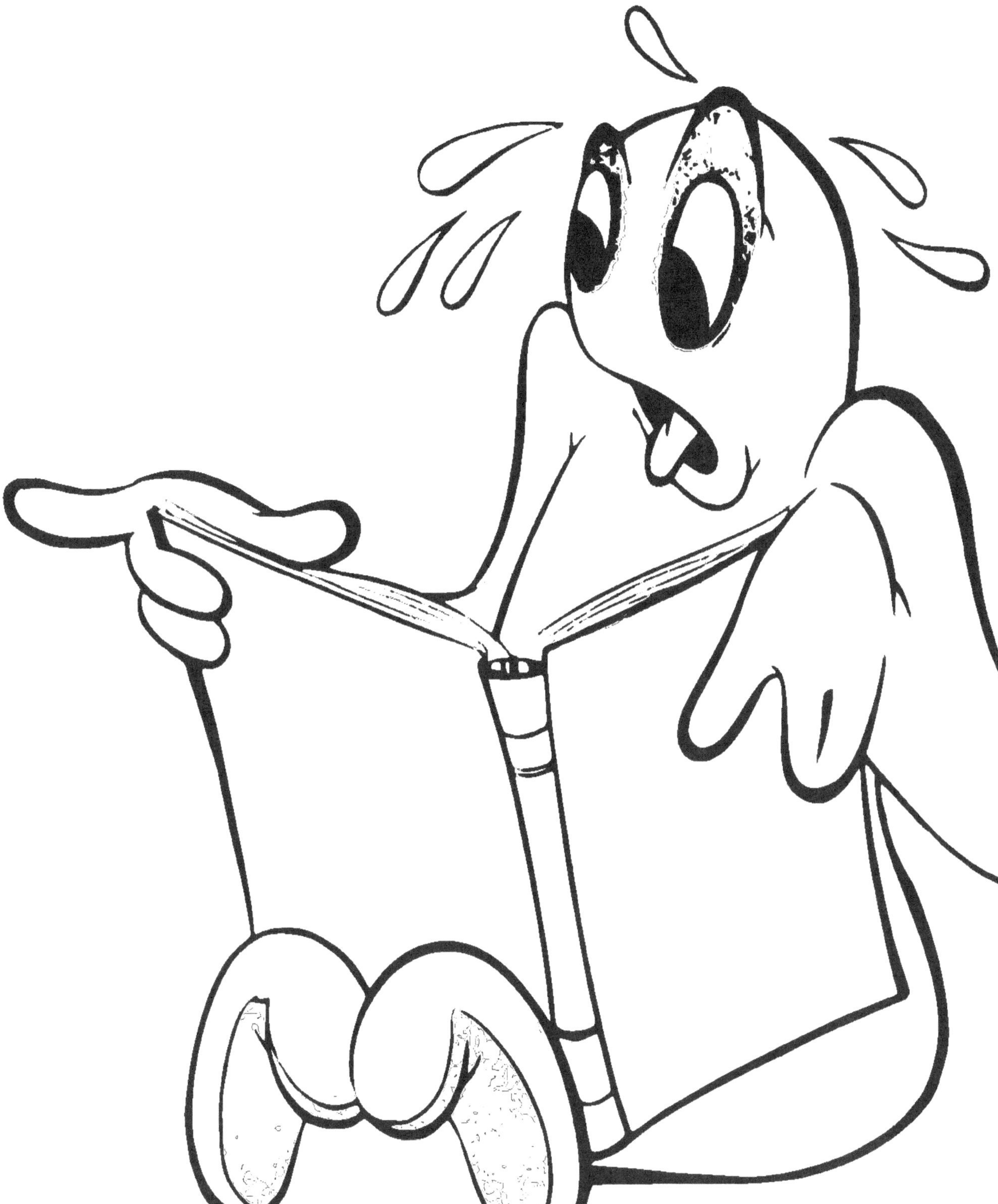

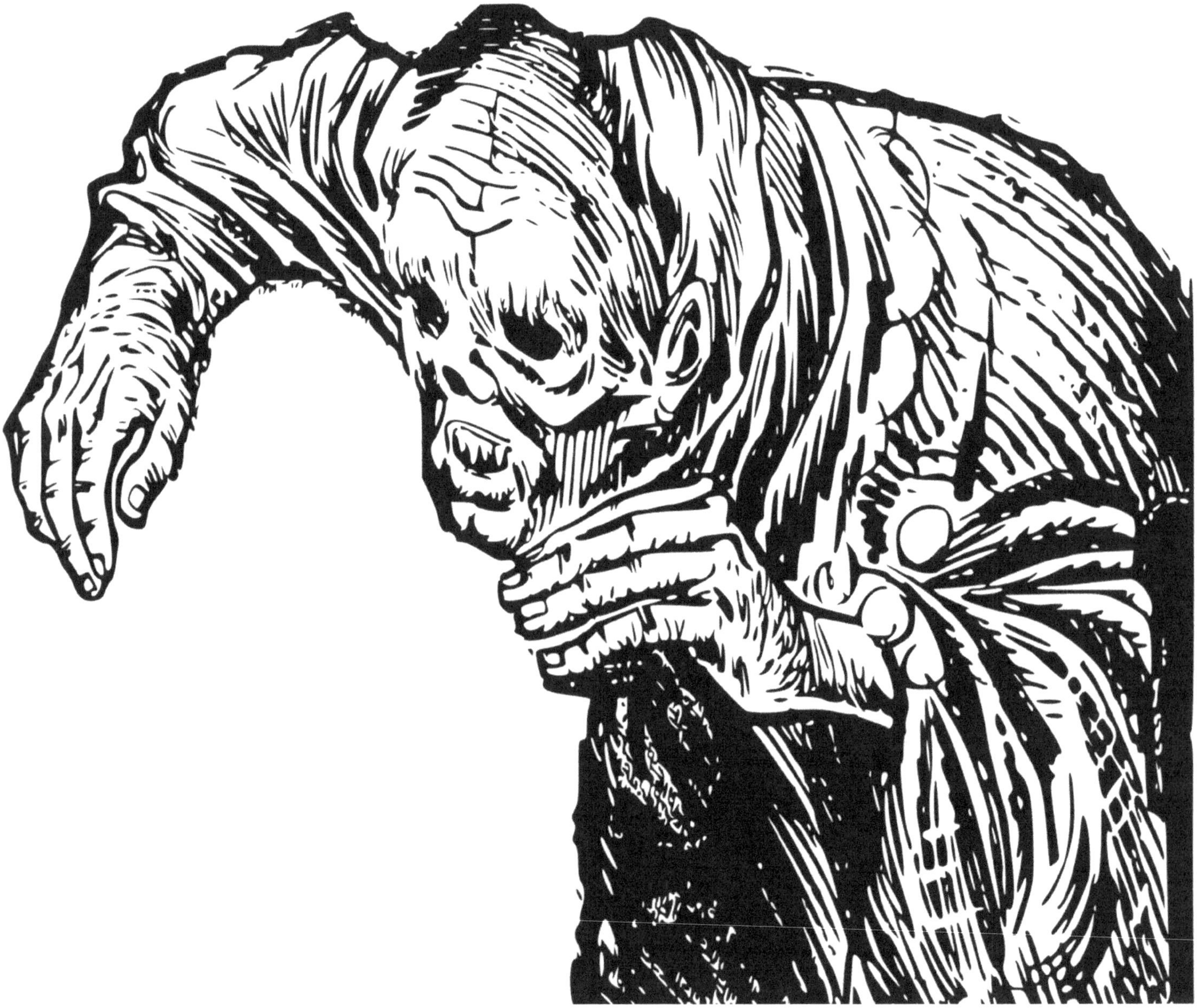

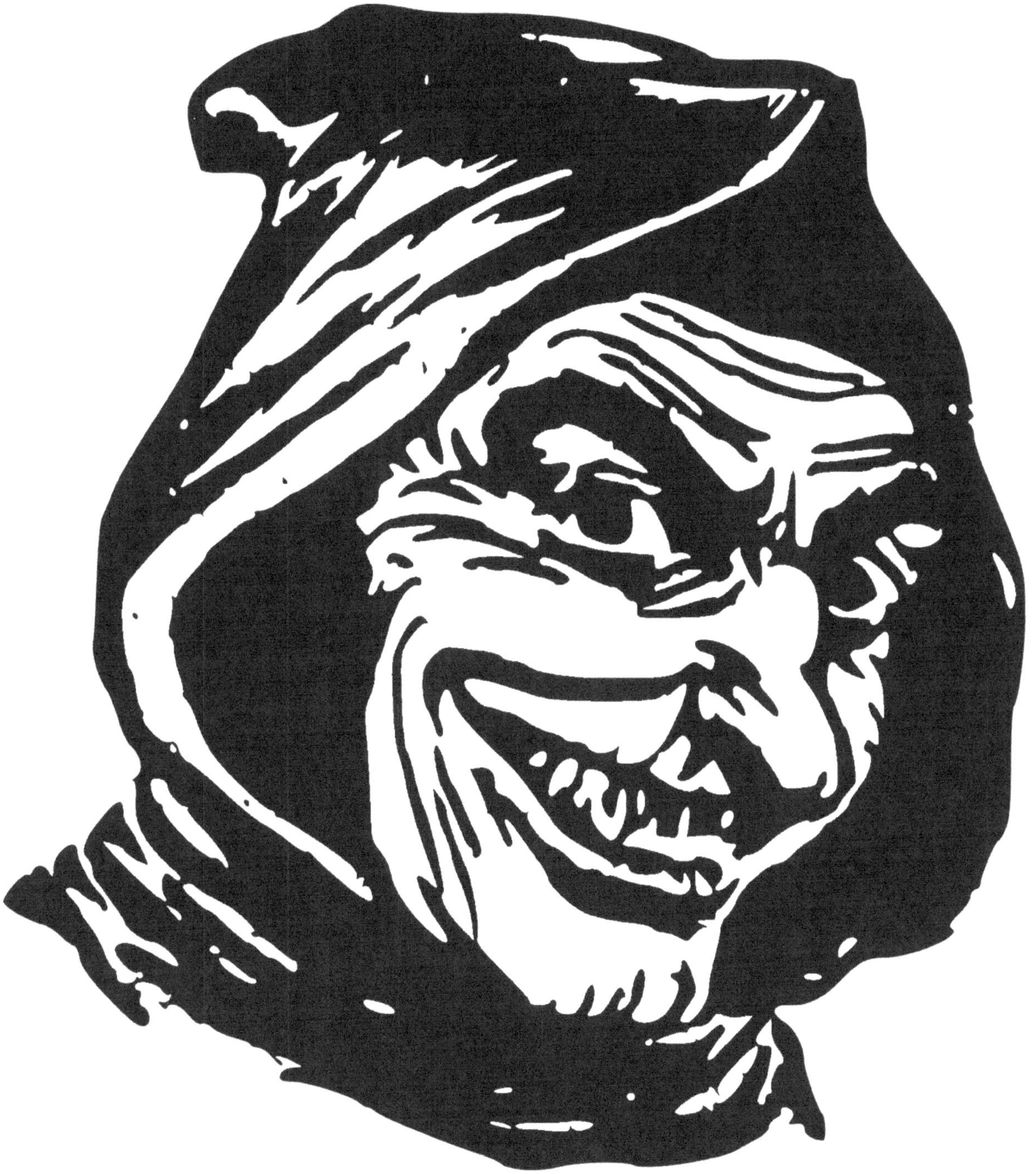

www.ingramcontent.com/pod-product-compliance
Lightning Source LLC
Chambersburg PA
CBHW081823170526
45167CB00008B/3525
* 9 7 8 1 5 4 2 9 1 6 5 0 9 *